D1242503

DOG BREEDS

# Doberman Pinschers

by Sara Green

Consultant:
Michael Leuthner, D.V.M.
Petcare Animal Hospital
Madison, Wisc.

BELLWETHER MEDIA • MIN

Note to Librarians, Teachers, and Parents:

**Blastoff! Readers** are carefully developed by literacy experts and combine standards-based content with developmentally appropriate text.

**Level 1** provides the most support through repetition of high-frequency words, light text, predictable sentence patterns, and strong visual support.

**Level 2** offers early readers a bit more challenge through varied simple sentences, increased text load, and less repetition of high-frequency words.

**Level 3** advances early-fluent readers toward fluency through increased text and concept load, less reliance on visuals, longer sentences, and more literary language.

**Level 4** builds reading stamina by providing more text per page, increased use of punctuation, greater variation in sentence patterns, and increasingly challenging vocabulary.

**Level 5** encourages children to move from "learning to read" to "reading to learn" by providing even more text, varied writing styles, and less familiar topics.

Whichever book is right for your reader, Blastoff! Readers are the perfect books to build confidence and encourage a love of reading that will last a lifetime!

This edition first published in 2011 by Bellwether Media, Inc.

No part of this publication may be reproduced in whole or in part without written permission of the publisher. For information regarding permission, write to Bellwether Media, Inc., Attention: Permissions Department, 5357 Penn Avenue South, Minneapolis, MN 55419.

Library of Congress Cataloging-in-Publication Data

Green, Sara, 1964–
  Doberman pinschers / by Sara Green.
    p. cm. – (Blastoff! readers: Dog breeds)
  Includes bibliographical references and index.
  Summary: "Simple text and full-color photography introduce beginning readers to the characteristics of the dog breed Doberman Pinschers. Developed by literacy experts for students in kindergarten through third grade"–Provided by publisher.
  ISBN 978-1-60014-459-2 (hardcover : alk. paper)
  1. Doberman pinscher–Juvenile literature. I. Title.

SF429.D6G74 2010
  636.73'6–dc22                                    2010000675

Printed in the United States of America, North Mankato, MN.

080110      1162

# Contents

# What Are Doberman Pinschers?

Doberman Pinschers are strong dogs with smooth **coats**. They are also called Dobermans or Dobies. Some people believe the Doberman **breed** looks unfriendly. However, most Dobermans are friendly and smart.

Dobermans are 24 to 28 inches (61 to 71 centimeters) tall. They weigh 66 to 88 pounds (30 to 40 kilograms). The Doberman breed is a member of the **Working Group** of dogs.

Most Doberman coats are reddish or black in color. Some Doberman coats are light tan, or fawn. All Dobermans have tan markings on their coats. They have marks on their **muzzles**, chests, legs, and feet. They also have markings above their eyes and under their tails.

Dobermans are born with floppy ears and long tails. Some owners like the look of pointed ears and short tails.

**Veterinarians** can give Dobermans an operation to make their ears stand up. Veterinarians can also **dock** Doberman tails. However, many owners let their Dobermans keep their floppy ears and long tails.

# History of Doberman Pinschers

Louis Dobermann was a tax collector in Germany in the late 1800s. He often carried a lot of money. He needed a guard dog to protect him from thieves. He wanted a dog breed that was loyal, strong, and intelligent. Louis did not think such a breed existed in Germany.

## fun fact

"Pinscher" is the German word for "terrier." Louis Dobermann originally wanted to breed a large terrier.

Manchester Terrier

Louis also worked at a dog pound. He knew which breeds had **traits** he wanted in a guard dog. He decided to **crossbreed** several types of dogs. These included the German Pinscher, Rottweiler, and Manchester Terrier.

In the late 1800s, a **litter** of puppies was born that had the traits Louis wanted. Louis' friends gave the new breed his name.

Rottweiler

German Pinscher

Dobermans became well known during World War I. They served as messenger dogs and search and rescue dogs for the German military.

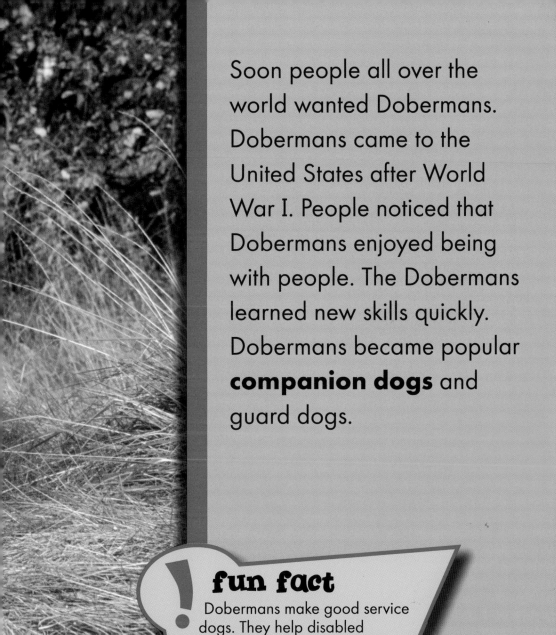

Soon people all over the world wanted Dobermans. Dobermans came to the United States after World War I. People noticed that Dobermans enjoyed being with people. The Dobermans learned new skills quickly. Dobermans became popular **companion dogs** and guard dogs.

**fun fact**

Dobermans make good service dogs. They help disabled people with everyday tasks.

In the 1940s, the United States military trained Dobermans to help World War II soldiers. The Dobermans worked as messengers and scouts.

25 MARINE WAR DOGS GAVE THEIR LIVES LIBERATING
GUAM IN 1944. THEY SERVED AS SENTRIES, MESSENGERS, SCOUTS.
THEY EXPLORED CAVES, DETECTED MINES AND BOOBY TRAPS.
SEMPER FIDELIS

| KURT | YONNIE | KOKO | BUNKIE |
| SKIPPER | PONCHO | TUBBY | HOBO |
| NIG | PRINCE | FRITZ | EMMY |
| MISSY | CAPPY | DUKE | MAX |
| BLITZ | ARNO | SILVER | BROCKIE |
| BURSCH | PEPPER | LUDWIG | RICKEY |

TAM (BURIED AT SEA OFF ASAN POINT)

GIVEN IN THEIR MEMORY AND ON BEHALF OF THE SURVIVING MEN
OF THE 2nd AND 3rd MARINE WAR DOG PLATOONS, MANY OF WHOM
OWE THEIR LIVES TO THE BRAVERY·AND SACRIFICE OF THESE
GALLANT ANIMALS
BY WILLIAM W. PUTNEY DVM C.O. 3rd DOG PLATOON
DEDICATED THIS DAY 21 JULY 1994

The military wanted to honor the brave
Dobermans after the war ended. They put a
statue of a Doberman at the U.S. Naval base
in Guam. The statue is called *Always Faithful*.

# Doberman Pinschers Today

## ! fun fact

Doberman Pinschers do well on dog intelligence tests. They are considered one of the smartest dog breeds.

Dobermans still help people today. Some Dobermans train to be search and rescue dogs. They help find missing people. Search and rescue Dobermans pick up a missing person's scent. They follow it with their noses until they find the person. They can even follow a scent through a crowd of people!

Many Dobermans and their owners participate in a sport called **agility**. In agility, dogs race through an obstacle course. The obstacles include tunnels, jumps, and ramps. The dog that finishes fastest with the fewest mistakes wins!

Dobermans are loyal companions. They love to learn new skills. You can have a lot of fun with a Doberman!

# Glossary

**agility**—a dog sport where dogs run through a series of obstacles

**breed**—a type of dog

**coats**—the hair or fur of animals

**companion dogs**—dogs that provide friendship to people

**crossbreed**—to mate different dog breeds together to make a new breed

**dock**—to shorten the tail of a dog

**litter**—a group of young; puppies in a litter are born to one mother at the same time.

**muzzles**—the noses, jaws, and mouths of animals

**traits**—characteristics of an animal

**veterinarians**—doctors who take care of animals

**Working Group**—dog breeds that do jobs to help humans

# To Learn More

**AT THE LIBRARY**
American Kennel Club. *The Complete Dog Book for Kids*. New York, N.Y.: Howell Books, 1996.

Fiedler, Julie. *Doberman Pinschers*. New York, N.Y.: PowerKids Press, 2006.

Stone, Lynn M. *Dobermans*. Vero Beach, Fla.: Rourke Publishing, 2007.

**ON THE WEB**
Learning more about Doberman Pinschers is as easy as 1, 2, 3.

1. Go to www.factsurfer.com.

2. Enter "Doberman Pinschers" into the search box.

3. Click the "Surf" button and you will see a list of related Web sites.

With factsurfer.com, finding more information is just a click away.

# Index

The images in this book are reproduced through the courtesy of: Debbi Smirnoff, front cover; J. Harrison/ KimballStock, pp. 4-5, 10-11, Nick Ridley/Photolibrary, p. 6 (small), 20; James Brey, pp. 6-7, 21; Verena Scholze/Alamy, p. 8; Pavel Shlykov/Alamy, p. 9; Cherry Hills/Photolibrary, p. 12; Juan Martinez, p. 13 (Rottweiler); Juniors Bildarchiv/Alamy, p. 13 (German Pinscher); Faith A. Uridel/KimballStock, pp. 14-15; ClassicStock/Masterfile, p. 16; Photri/Topham/The Image Works, p. 17; Jim West/Age Fotostock, pp. 18-19.